Caroline

LOGORRHEA DEMENTIA

OTHER TITLES BY KYLE DARGAN

The Listening (University of Georgia Press, 2004)
Bouquet of Hungers (University of Georgia Press, 2007)

THE

V Q R

POETRY
SERIES

Logorrhea Dementia

[~ A SELF–DIAGNOSIS ~]

POEMS BY KYLE DARGAN

The University of Georgia Press   Athens and London

Published by The University of Georgia Press
Athens, Georgia 30602
www.ugapress.org
© 2010 by Kyle Dargan
All rights reserved
Designed by Mindy Basinger Hill
Set in 10.5/15 Minion Pro
Printed and bound by Thomson-Shore
The paper in this book meets the guidelines for
permanence and durability of the Committee on
Production Guidelines for Book Longevity of the
Council on Library Resources.

Printed in the United States of America
14   13   12   11   10   P   5   4   3   2   1

Library of Congress Cataloging-in-Publication Data
Dargan, Kyle.
Logorrhea dementia : a self-diagnosis : poems / by Kyle Dargan.
     p.   cm.
ISBN-13: 978-0-8203-3684-8 (pbk. : alk. paper)
ISBN-10: 0-8203-3684-X (pbk. : alk. paper)
I. Title.
PS3604.A74L64 2010
811'.6—dc22

                    2010009615

British Library Cataloging-in-Publication Data available

*Speaking a language is different from feeling it. One
Japanese woman says that when she swears in English,
she feels nothing.*
~ Elaine Equi

I'm American, honey. Our names don't mean shit.
~ Butch

*A man who has a language consequently possesses the
world expressed and implied by that language. What
we are getting at becomes plain: Mystery of language
affords remarkable power. Paul Valéry knew this, for he
called language "the god gone astray in flesh."*
~ Frantz Fanon

I am still a raisin in the sun raging against the machine.
~ Lupe Fiasco

SYMPTOMS

[~ THIRDBREATH ~]

BREATHING: A PRELIMINARY

Think of the body as an endless call and response between oxygen and carbon dioxide. Think of blood as the medium and the messenger, blood as the place where words morph or vanish, blood as the impulse ("what did you say?") for necessary improvisation. When we see blood on the body, we believe we know it well: another one of the body's pleas for attention—a holler. But such are the misconceptions of the eyes.

* * *

Three years ago, a friend—fellow poet, a blues man—telephoned me from the midwestern state university where he was teaching to vent about a graduate student of his who could not hear him. He was suggesting a title for the student's MFA thesis, but the student could not hear it. He called me, told me the title, and asked me to assure him that he was not the deaf one. He wasn't. There was a music in the phrase, a thrust that made use of our tongues. But it was such an available and obvious music that—despite whatever toll the graduate student's stubbornness or the drabness of that college town had taken on him—I knew he didn't need me to corroborate his hearing. That wasn't what the phone call was truly about. Unsatisfied and still weary after my reassurance, my friend confessed, "You know what it is? I'm just tired of writing poems that make sense." Beyond saying, "I know what you mean," I could not articulate to him that I in fact did understand. My ears translated his lament as, "I'm tired of writing the poems I'm expected to write and whose language leads me to the places I'm expected to go." I too once found myself in a similar space, though it was a different college town in a different midwestern state. Maybe I am still a runagate from that place. Maybe that is why I couldn't remember or explain to him how I crawled out of it.

* * *

At some point after escaping the larynx, breath becomes a body—engorged with itself and free of the cells that compose our flesh. To this breath language will attach itself—a fickle symbiote, a fellow fugitive.

ACKNOWLEDGMENTS

Versions of these poems have appeared in the following journals:

Beltway Poetry Quarterly: "Men Die Miserably for Lack"

Black Renaissance / Renaissance Noire: "The Burning of a Black Hero and a Dawn (1971)," "Flight School," and "Harmonica, Green Line"

Cavalier Magazine: "For a Fee," "A History of Fear," "No Passengers," and "Sex with America"

Drunken Boat: "How to Lick a Blade"

Foreign Policy in Focus: "Pilot to Bombardier"

jubilat: "Entropy" and "Star-Spangled Sutra"

Poet Lore: "Deciduous Youths"

Shenandoah: "Letter Home No. 3"

Tuesday Journal: "Equinox"

"Entropy" first appeared in the Cave Canem 10 x 10 series.

"[Habeas Corpus]" first appeared in the anthology *Cut Loose the Body*, edited by Rose Berger and Joseph Ross.

"Man of the Family" first appeared in *Writing the Self and the Community: African American Poetry after the Civil Rights Movement* (Norton), edited by Charles Henry Rowell.

I would like to extend my immense thanks to Erika Stevens for her interest, foresight, craftiness, and patience during the completion of this manuscript.

[~ FIRSTBREATH ~]

Entropy

~ for Theresa

What if our alphabet was full
of atoms :: I would speak in moles—
spill more in my sleep than a drunk
criers' convention :: *Hear Ye,*
I could not be silent :: Silence translates
into all things and nothings
like the atom in fission
labs—atomic models braced
on wooden bones :: If atoms
left fossils, they would be etchings,
an ornate script illegible
across all our faces—

You Lost Your Heart in Manhattan

By the time a guttersweep retrieved the muscle,
it had become a grid of one-way sinews.

Every lover from that moment on you needed
to warn *it just takes time. Make enough wrong turns
and you learn what goes uptown and what bleeds
toward the river.* One lover returned
claiming that your heart was his land
once bartered for gunpowder
and oxen head, that he'd trekked
halfway to Oklahoma before he knew
he'd been swindled.

But that history is no business of yours.

I'll See It When I Believe It

Ninety-eight percent of people will
die some time in their lives.
~ Ricky Bobby

Statistically, one can
prove airplane commutes
to be safer than train travel.
But the statistician fancies
walking to work, as on foot
he is 3.5 times more likely
to meet the potential mother
of his potential children.
Remembering this, he can only muster
a smile for every fourth woman
with whom he manages to share eyes.
At the bread shop, he forces
a stare through the baker's lenses,
yet he longs to decipher her hands,
to know if their powder is sweet
or chalky, though, statistically speaking,
incorporating food into pro-
creation is a poor idea.
We actually all taste alike
when fricasseed in life's ancient roux,
though, statistically, fewer perish
from hunger than specific thirsts
in this world draped with water.
While all data suggests more sinners
walk among us than in hell,
where no pencils endure
and the dead have never bothered
to return the surveys.

Dear R

Somewhere: a loom in a fallow
cotton field. There a farmer and her husband
watch the slack-jawed road,
awaiting the carrier's moped
carrying their odd bounty—boxes of hearts,
some packed in denim scraps,
others with straw.
                              The postman waits
while the husband wrings some blood
from each beating handful onto the plowed rows
before the hearts are repackaged,
returned to senders.

    *

In four months, a parcel arrives
—maybe just weeks or days
too late. Inside, a white spool
and a note jotted in the farmer's craggy script:
This is the thread of your blood.
Use it to bind what you fear
is unraveling—barely enough there
to suture a smirk of a wound.

    *

From an innocent fabric—blue water,
bubbles, and ducklings—you sewed a small
pocket, stuffed it with firm, synthetic down.
You promised me all I needed to know
percolated within that softness
I wasn't to tear into, but, if rested
beneath my ear, might speak to me.

But it held its plush tongue
while you and I continued to fray.

*

So my incision was small—enough
for my finger to scope the pillow's belly.
I sliced again, widening the portal
to find this thing you thought would save us
four years ago: a note,
like the farmer's—reading
. . . *always will*—but
there was no spooled blood.

*

This *love* you spoke of, is it akin to waiting
in a room as your heart
rests in the carriage of some courier's moped
with no idea of what will be sent in return
or if the return address is still true?

No Passengers

The already beautiful do not, as a rule, run.
I am at the moment seated.
~ Donald Barthelme

Please remain beautiful in the event
of emergency. Keep all limbs

and loose dreams behind the yellow
line. The next train on this track

will not stop—doors will stay pursed
as a phalanx of wheels shrieks by. Again

this train will take no passengers
but I—scores of myself:

some with folios, some with pockets
full of music, some mosaiced

with uncertainty, some with gun barrels
clamped between damp waistbands

and the smalls of backs. Each me
related by motion more than quiddity

—we move. All desirous of *up* but
willing to settle for *forward* today.

Please remain beautiful
as this train passes—only gorgeous stasis

guarantees that the winds
from our escape will pith you

humane and clean. In departing,
we bequeath to you a final sight—

this smear of glass and steel flashed
like cellulose skimming a light unknown.

The Most Beautiful City in the Wounded Empire

They've refaced the license plates.
Soon, none will recall
when Liberty's oxidized green
dermis and dress were our symbols
for this beautiful city (now with new
laws dictating all scurry outside
to stuff smoke in their mouths).

The colors, you say (the drowned
sepia circling the models' eyes).
Worn to stucco, the posters on sidewalk
plywood carousels move when we do.
Pedestrians move when the cars
move—cutting against each other
like virgins tumescent with pride.

Why do you love this place? I'm from
New Jersey. When you say, *the city*,
I think of tunnels, still armadas
of brake lights. I think
of a place called home and reasons
to go there. And you? These days
you want to come with me.

Equinox

~ *Penn Station, Newark, New Jersey*

Spring sashays off the Transit train to *oyes* and *aquís*. A mocking boy clutches his breast as if he's seen Mary, calling her name—*Mami de Dios*—desire's crude self-crucifixion. He will not die here. His heart staggers into a jazzed procession of porters in uniforms full—purple, maroon with succulent tassel braids and white gloves that perch like angels on their shoulders. Winter died like a hard-headed piano solo, had to perish so that Spring could dust off her black mini—hem risen like the barometric pressure, her dew point almost visible between strides. It isn't supposed to rain this weekend. That's what the weather report said. That's when it usually pours.

Harmonica, Green Line

He plays with muted shoulder
movement.
                                  He plays with
       a seesaw
progression as I pass
L'Enfant Plaza (*wrong
fucking train*)—listening.

He plays with this captive
audience—blows sharp notes,
then lifts to peer outside
the paused metro car,
then sits down, blows soft.

He prays his play.

He plays for no one except *he*,
his mouth's steady resuscitation
of that black breath box—
a cassette tape swelled
with CO_2 and whatever
a harmonica man won't speak.

All of it moist
like the under-crux
of where the jaw ends
and where sound is
simple and famished.

Wandered, The

~ Glover Park, Washington, D.C.

Tucked under the pre-dawn silence,
there is a boy laid like garnish on the raw
sidewalk—some measure of dead I assume.
I learn to walk as my neighbors would: stepping
a sharp arc out and around his splayed legs.

Even in winter's steady palm,
he seems not to pulse. The stone beneath
his head bears nothing but his head—
maybe sleep, but no sign
that I should risk his waking.
I alert no one—let the breathless lay
at 3 a.m. Enter your house, lock your door,
and maybe thumb your memory for prayers.

      Likely, the call comes in
      from the mother in the house
      behind the tree
      beneath which this unknown sleeps.
Police lights' familiar searing drags me
through my window curtains—anxious to witness
how such things unfold in Georgetown.
A voice, distorted by the cruiser PA, calls
"Sir, please move." *Fools, he is no more.*
"Sir, you need to move." There is no third
warning. I fear they will come
knocking for information, alibis. I'll say
ask the stone—the only thing on the block
that dares listen to him, consider his weight.
Instead, they slide out from the cruiser,
rouse him with a shake, and lead him
slowly into the patrol car
like coroners of dreams.

[~ SECONDBREATH ~]

Infomercial Soliloquy against Apocalypse

A pizza slice has forced me to ponder
the red onion's necessity,
the *ifs* of its being. Difficult to imagine
some priest praying for red onions'
existence. It isn't like god
even takes requests anymore—this call-in show
taped ages ago, in endless rerun.

Maybe the "Big G" is a marketer
at heart—driven to see
if there is anything he can't sell
(Product of the Week: produce,
red onion). I was sold the idea
that god is male, that I'm not
chosen and thus his skin will never match
mine. Even if I could, I wouldn't choose
the guise of god. What kind of mirror-
masochist would one have to be?
Say, I'd loathe to look like Lebron
yet only be able to fly one foot off the ground—
people would always demand,
"Dunk, dunk," and I'd have to
spin excuses on my finger
like a ball, try to make slamming
down a wastebasket miraculous.
King James could even sue me
for soft defamation, like John Malkovich
in that movie about John Malkovich
that really wasn't about John Malkovich.

God never saw a human being
or red onion he didn't like
because that is his job—a heart-to-heart
salesman knocking on your thorax,
carrying an attaché of something
you've just got to try.

Ooth Jazz

A good song can enter
church sweaty
—sea-skinned—
can wake Sunday
morning still swollen
from having been sliced
in the wee hours
by a blade dipped
in curiosity, the notes
replicating like antibodies.

A good song can croon
god being that same love
whollified by two. It moans
for salvation's on-time arrival
and awaits the organ's throat singing
with penitence. A good song
is song, neither father nor son
nor mother. It is the Rubik's
of a zygote   turning-turning,
straining to decide
which of its faces will be blue.

Sex with America

My love for you makes all your lies seem true.
~ Marvin Gaye

I don't blame myself for being
unable to resist your synergy,
the *all-in* of a Republic—all owners
of their own flesh's land
tendered a vote and a role
to play. Someone to tweak *this*.
Someone to tongue *that*.
Our sweat defines the borders
when bodies press against bodies
like nations—one too weak
for struggle, one too large
to be sated with pleasure, one
with a nasal accent that sours
sweet talk. I can do without
truth from now on, Love.
Or rather, I won't have you
kiss me with catalytic lips.
But kiss me. Annex me, then feign
it never occurred. The oral
histories I carried to your lap
will never withstand the agile
crush of your pneumatic pelvis
(full   then empty   then
full), this hyperbaric longing. My love
for country leaves me breathless

—all this screaming
just to be heard over the moans
of others like me squeezed
between a welding sensation
and the discomfort of a destiny
united.

Dalmatian Syndrome

A priest convinced me jealousy was God's
only flaw. This was middle school, a phase
when I was oft reminded how odd I was
for harboring no lust for Madonna.
I had a history of such behavior.
EXHIBIT: an afternoon trek as adolescent
freight on our summer camp's aging bus
whose masochistic shocks
sought potholes. Inside, I sat dazed
while a little blonde girl puckered
kissy sounds, asking *Does that
give you a boner?* It hurt to tell her
no, as though I was proving
my malcalibrated desire—
her expression miffed, brow
caved like how I imagined Jesus
might cave when we hear *Madonna*
and conjure *Material Girl* before virgin mother.

Back then, any eye could see the lamb
in Leon's "Like a Prayer" reincarnation,
the soft propaganda of his lips
on Madonna's brow and cheek.
Such video miracle was no solace
from the news' nightly inoculations of black male
menace, no cover from my cousin's
leaden-heart pleas: *Kyle, promise me
you'll never date a white girl.*
What *ism*, what *syndrome*, do I claim?

Madonna has turned fifty,
and I find her attractive
for her age—her limbs' taut
language. Her body's symbol less
libido fodder. Less at stake
when someone shoves me magazines
asking if she is still *hot*.
Who is any one thing for all time?
Some mornings, I still believe
I am *black*. In reality, I flicker
like the streetlamp outside my bedroom—
its light sensor unsure if it is
still night. But it's dawn, overcast—a sunrise
behind the tree and cloud canopy, a shine that's there
even when we can't see it.

A Dark Age

This morning I woke wanting my neighbor
to walk my Heart to the scorched horizon
and, once their whistling grew faint,
blast out the back of its skull.

I handed him bills wrapped
in wax like yellow American
and asked he ask no questions.
"So done."

I then called Persephone back, let her in—felt
feet descending my chest cavity
toward a refurbished Hades.

My skin grew dark, the lashes
fell away from my eyes.
You could not tell my face
from a mud lake mute with frost.

Sound Culture

No one will be heard who does not speak in short bursts of truth.
~ Saul Bellow (as quoted by Bill Moyers)

I cannot be understood in three minutes.
~ Sidney Poitier

Blah-blah's pollen drifts from the trees,
inflames throats and ear canals—
narrows our portals for meaning.

Let us strip our words' syllables—shave serifs
from letters, slick down accent marks
so a molecule of script and sound can pass through
fiber-optic cable's thin esophagus:

Every story ever narrated
whittled down to "The End"—
some unnamed Ishmael mumbling
about a sea we won't know from sangria
or a whale we can no longer discern
from a fruit chunk wedged in the mouth
of history's half-empty carafe.

Penny Therapy

~for those whose text messages I occasionally ignore

One August, your grandfather was born a fish
in a flooded stone quarry.

He dreaded drainage,
eloped with evolution,

and the rest is . . .
what do they call it? Anyway,

I'm trying to explain that you too
were born in that place.

Dying there would be plebian.

Swim against it,
your undertow of apprehension.

To die there would be to die
as mere banter. Die distant,

or die where you are—
worth merely your weight in pixels.

Past Parallax

Last night, I made love to a star. Pristine,
the sky. Blustery. I climbed
a staircase of wind from my window
to soft-step across
the ozone's crumbling balcony.

She was draped in eon's
old light, picking the bones
of cosmonauts from her braids.
I knelt, hugged her
midsection, pressed my cheek
over her belly's cool plane.
Though barren, she was motherly
in that moment before she unwrapped
the luminance from her shoulders,
and we fumbled for each other
in the cherry darkness.

Through sleep, I reached for the pen, paused:
another poem, another phantom longing.
What will critics think of these
once I'm gone. That I was hijacked
by the carnal, blood thin with youth?
No, it's that I fall in love with people
so far from the ground beneath me
I feel the span as measurable
only in light and years.

Ask the Devil

~ for Torshana

Ask the Devil, and he'll share
his resentment—swear to you he's never
beaten his wife, not the sun-shower type.
"Thunder," he might explain,
"is the sound of giant sheets
beaten out after love's tumbles"—a bed
smoothed into blue heavens.

For lightning, there is no euphemism.
"To wield ignorance, one must suffer
some of its affliction," he'll say. His way
of admitting he's no different than you or I
—just dumb and fascinated
with lightning's bright, stabbing
fissures. Remember, you and I
beneath the porch's wing,
watching flashes echo
while rain pulverized the pansies.
Jagged light. Our eyes still
gaping when the storm slammed
closed a vacuum of burnt air
and the clap threw me back
against the screen door. My face
and ear numb from the sky's wallop.
You laughed like the Devil—
wise enough to know
there's no safe count of seconds
between lightning and thunder
when you stand so close to the surge.

Jesus in the Yucatan

bleeds from the wrists, ankles.
Paint chips from his brow
onto a newspaper photo
of a fútbol trinity—three dark-haired
players vying for a header.

From ribs and abdomen, red paint
seeps—these parts no more
than smoky shading on terra cotta.

Not a Mayan feature to his name—this savior
who saves us from difference
among the twenty faces
of the Aztec calendar,
among the jaguars and obsidian
idols replete with misfortune.

"Carry me from here," pleads the lord,
but tourists pass him—Yanks
and Brits disinterested in his familiar
visage. They opt for gilded
calligraphy hung from their necks,
symbols and glyphs to smuggle home.
They long for their hearts' quickening
with tremors of discovery,
plunder's forgotten palpitations.

Tauromachia

Today, you are the bull
and I the espada. You will be
bled for the oil
of your aggression engine,
you dark, dense thing.
Sharp-headed. A lance, but much
more stubborn. The picador
out of horn's reach. The crowd's
arms churning like the cranks
of unfed grinders—the cheering
a mashing of air. I have no tongue,
no taste, for you. Ask the hollow
kiss you left in the matador's shoulder
what it knows of your heart's
cloistered wanting. *A sword impales, no?*
No. We are more than pageant.
When the lovers return home later,
pressing or impaling one another,
are they not thinking of how
I entered you—driven, diving
down into your aorta's stream?
Will they not reenact our brief
barbarism to warm their worlds?

Conflict Chic

~ for Tala

All around you are lands where the word
tomorrow vapors at room temperature.
You speak it to a woman crumpled
against a blast wall. *Idiot* she snaps at you,
serrated and vexed. She sends you home,
tailbone tucked even deeper, to ponder if you are
one of those people who loves to wear scarves
woven of another's victimhood—
solidarity's checkered knit stretched
thin as a finish line? You don't know
the first thing about suffering.
But you're pro-something. You know that much.
Even if a thing is only your own neck.

Men Die Miserably for Lack

*When a dog bites a man, that is not news, because it
happens so often. But if a man bites a dog, that is news.*
~ John B. Bogart

Some of you are men. The remainder,
mutts who do not speak, who fetch
the morning sun with limber tongues
and barks like muted horns.
Unless struck in traffic, a dog dies
in private holds—transitioned
from *alive* to *unseen*, barely
a tally. When hunger bites
the expected, when blind rockets
dismember the expected, call them
by their names. When a virus
hunkers in the expected's body,
when the written word remains
foreign to the expected's eyes, remember
their faces—chronically passé—
as this is all news of the dogs.
No ink will be shed for them. Their press
conferences will be small circles
inscribed with howls, limp tails,
and clawed clay. In a blue rage,
in fear, a dog may bite
a dog—which is less than news,
less than assumption. "Reality," it is.
"Sad" even. Neither pause the printers
nor pique our heart's Nielsen ratings.

Men are news. When man
bites dog—his teeth, blackened
with headlines, breaking skin—
only then will the dog become news,
become man—worthy, dying, and worthy.

In Praise of Jailbreaks

This is no absolution for what you may do

once caught within the rapture of uncaged air.

If yours was trespass through data ports, through kitchen windows,

or through the ear or eye into the psyche—such treading

dead-ends in punitive soil.   This you knew.

But for your trespass into the world of the free

—via digging, via disguises, via a heart's hydraulic

push, via thumbs flicking against guards' gun holsters—

you earn beauty. That you escape walls enclosed by walls,

driven by fishnet vistas and a porous metal plane,

makes you angel—contracted to eviscerate

the larynx of human arrogance.

Your shank-scribbled adieu: *Man was not meant to pen*

man. Complicity, the only sound prison. And again, I desire this.

Who would I be offering you forgiveness?

Gazelle Theory No. 44

You're a gazelle . . . and here comes a lion!
~ from Warner Brothers cartoon

In a field of yet harvested hands
chapped by winds of disbelief,
an idea named "Blackness"—a deep
charcoal smudge against the plains—grazes.
The idea, it shifts its weight
in slow-shutter blurs—wispy animal chassis
spread about in blots of *was* and *is*.

The field of hands preys on the idea's
afterimages, devours each new and fleeting
form as though gobbling husks of light.

Endangered,
the idea gorges, then escapes—
careful not to rest
its soft hooves too long
lest a print be left
for those even hungrier to follow.

The Burning of a Black Hero and a Dawn (1971)

~ The old Loew's Theatre, Newark, New Jersey

Someone shouts BOMB (though it is
only a canister of flames). The theatre
rips away from the feature before Roundtree can

embody Shaft. All scream. My grandmother
(the detective), my young aunt (the brains) jump
into good-cop / not-cop roles. Grandmother drags

my aunt toward fire exits, trampled by shadows
along the way. America screams for the black hero
to skin himself of tight trousers and unleash

his coil—that long nether-tongue fluent
only in stereotypes—and lay into *the man*
and *the man*'s doe Janes, swift. My aunt catches

glimpses of the screen, realizes there is nothing
projected they need to flee: "Everyone is running
this way, Mama. Can't we go another?"

Love lubricates reason, and they pivot together
to ease out the theatre's main door. Neither knows
how *Shaft* ends, but two escaped into a new day.

I know. I've seen them—mother and daughter, survivors
of their own people's fear of flat images.

Try Again

You say "hints of flesh"
as though nudity were some riddle.
"Guess," says the nape, the tummy,
the calves. "*Need* is not the answer,
numbnuts," your high-school-wrestling-coach
-slash-freshman-health-teacher might say.

But you can retake these quizzes
each day you board a train, seduced
by the passing of bodies eager to be
not-bodies but translucent mannequins.
(*Nothing to see here. Look
through me. Move along.*)

After another C-, you could care less.
"Guess," says the collarbone,
the triceps. But, exhausted,
you reply, "Go fuck yourself"—imploring skin
to do the only thing it succeeds at
more than obscuring our bodies' secrets
beneath its chapped trust.

For a Fee

I will undress and wire-stitch
your quilt of needs to mine—
fly the impromptu banner
from my spine's flagpole.

For one fee, I'll prop myself
before reality's video cameras
until I'm famous for breathing.
But for more, a next trick
—I'll swan dive
and seat myself
on a fish tank's floor
while water subdues my lungs.
Rest me for one day
atop my revenue's palate,
then shroud and ship my body
to my mother. For a fee,
of course, I expect you would
write her my death notice.
Tell her I died
saving you all from drowning—
that beneath water I spun
then stilled slowly
like a coin
dropped on its side.

[~ THIRDBREATH ~]

O for Operator

We'd like to be connected to
the Office of Offhand Brilliance
so we may register a quip
cousin Clem—from Murfreesboro—
opined over creamed corn and venison.

While we dined, minds gnawing on our universe's
constant expansion, Clem says: "It's like
a too-deep hunger—by the time you feed it
it's already outgrown the meal."

Hello?

If this request cannot be honored, connect us
to the poet laureate's office so we might breathe
heavily into the receiver until he hangs up
or, frothing, demands to know our names.

Deciduous Youths

Tequan achieved liftoff one afternoon,
his skate-clad feet rising only to crash
while racing to our launch—the scrape
a wild, bloody leaf on his shin.

We had to persist without him.

Under our low-top fades
and the soft knots of adolescent minds,
we thought we were reptilian—that any limb
lost to the scorched holler of an M–80
would regenerate with time.

              Neighbors couldn't decide
if we were art or anarchy. It did not matter.
We snatched matches from parents' dressers,
went to find the things that would fly
once we put flame to them—Roman candles,
bottle rockets, wailing wheels
that spark-spun in place, hypnotic as chrome
car rims that would entice our generation
some ten years later, piercing
as the sound of Tequan's screams
when his mother doused his wound with green
alcohol two blocks away. Even for his horror
we could not pause—compelled to adorn the air
with our own burning, our own noise.

Public-Verb Agreement

~ ATLANTA, GEORGIA

All us we folk
person community first.
Invent truth,
~ Thomas Sayers Ellis

MARTA car windows laminate
East Point, trap the postindustrial
specimen. A spectre haunts
the rust, glares at our motion, whispers
as weeds swell in quick to blur
these razed factory foundations
before I can recall this was
America—our country once manufactured
here. The warehouses' checkered glass
cloaked in bloated graffiti:
"THE FINAL DAYS HAS ARRIVED!!"
—punk prophets with spray cans,
who asked you?

This brittling economy has made us
louder. The brother seated behind me
jabber-jaws on his cell phone, trying to woo
dinner from a woman he yearns to slip inside.
"Are you inviting me, though? I want
to hear you say it"—his cawed words
sprawl in every empty seat. More:
"What I tell you 'bout that negative tone,
woman? Don't give me that—
I don't care who you is."
(Can a recession turn on the pleasure
from food, hinge on how
we mold one another's egos?)

I'm hearing the dollar losing value around me.
I'm hearing one man hunger for another
body, but the voice at his line's end
has neither the patience nor the time.

Flight School

Gravity makes me want to float away
~ Joi

Sky-Rob's missteps were mythic. He once jumped and whacked a backboard with his skull. The story relayed among us with nervous laughs and fear of the truth in Sky-Rob's legs—what couldn't they do if he "applied himself," as school counselors woed. At track meets, he'd glide over high jump bars in seated posture—a quasi-gangster lean, his arm outstretched conjuring the plushed simplicity of girl's bubble vest in the phantom passenger's seat. Sky-Rob said very little, his body saving all breath for leaping, while his leaps said to hell with proper form. Whenever teachers or coaches told us there was a *right way* to the world, I thought of Sky-Rob in the air on nothing but pure, incalculable ability. I knew Sky-Rob would elevate one day and forget to descend, message us with graffiti tags on the clouds' underbellies, that he would rise above Irvington and all its gray and quick deaths. Then I see Sky-Rob on a Union Avenue corner, years after high school, clad in black from skull cap to toes. I shout, but he doesn't hear me. He doesn't even seem to move—those same legs inextricably grounded.

How to Lick a Blade

The tongue must flatten
like a child's palm turned open
by a mother's suspicion—

There must be nothing
there but appetite.

      With the slicing
edge turned from your face,
draw metal back against the taste
buds. As your mind
phantoms hints of blood
within flavors sought,
know you are not slit.

You taste the center
of something else severed.

Man of the Family

Your sister calls from college to say, "There's an asshole in my bed."
Usually, it was *under* and *a monster*. You realize a flashlight and the
can of air freshener that doubled as goblin repellant won't help this
situation. Think like a doctor, the asshole a condition: "When did you
first notice the asshole? How long has he been in your bed?" But such
histories no older brother desires to jot down. She begs you treat her
symptom with fists, lots of them. So you drive to your friends' homes
with a burlap sack, filling her prescription one rung doorbell at a time,
wishing your father's giant hands were still a mere shout away.

Letter Home No. 3

~ Gettysburg, Pennsylvania

Is apple butter as simple
as its name suggests, Mama?
If so, why is it sought after
as though it were a scarce salve
for the tasteless tongue?

No bother.

Twenty-five miles per hour, I drove
through the battlefields where
blue and gray bled—almost tears.
The piled stone walls, the rolling
openness. There was nothing
gray rebels could have hid behind
save another trembling body
or another ginned-up body,
while the round bullet feared not a soul.

At least that's how I imagine it.
There are only graves here, spires,
limestone hunks with bronze scabs
of history and grass
the color of spoiled regret.

And "Lincoln Square" is actually
a circle. Abe remains misunderstood.

Star-Spangled Sutra

If the weapon be a mask, sand down the dorsal self
        so the mask clings to nothing but the mask.

      *

If the weapon be holy, keep it oiled with doubt—
        the chamber, the forte, the bow's dark joy.

      *

If the weapon be human, draw ligaments snug
        over hollow joints—motion insulated, pooling
        like venom in limbs.

      *

If the weapon be utterance, fix its warhead
        against a knot of air just atop the throat's plummet.

      *

If the weapon be flame, first douse yourself
        with remorse. Distinguish your enemies. Ignite them.

[Habeas Corpus]

~ after Fernando Botero / Abu Ghraib

Information, its pome,
grows from the neck. String
the body bottom up
until this sprouts below clavicle:
head with a seed of speech
you wrap in scarlet rags
while it ripens—immersed
in its own denied senses.

What it cannot see, it will tell you
soon enough. What it cannot hear,
it will illustrate. Wait.

Cut loose the body. Tenderize
the flesh with baton and boot
licks until its own wine pools
about the fruit and blends
into the cloth's own red.

The human husks are to be
piled as a harvest mound, fertilized
and blessed with the hissing of bladders.
When a body can shiver no more,
it is time to peel back cloth
and listen as golden words
trickle from the lips.

This nectar, return it to your people.
Tell them—innocent, natural, as appetite
—we have information . . .

Pilot to Bombardier

Pilot to bombardier,
are the boulevards burning?
The out-of-Dodge roads? We feel
still heavy with payload,
though smoke whispers
of smoldering—of hamlets
and metropolises aflame.
Pilot to bombardier, I remember
kissing my wife in the hangar,
remember you brushing the bomb
like some mother delivering
her son to his first school day—
gravely aware the guidance
systems of his eyes would come
online after the short time
out of your arms, learning.
Pilot to bombardier (you would never
drop your child in a burning schoolhouse),
why are we flying, cradling meteoric clusters,
over lands already bursting with war-
heads and small-arms fire
and child soldiers and students
of battle and all their constant hopes
that the blast we carry might be
the one to eradicate enemy and enemy
alike?—a shockwave to slow all
air and artillery until they drop
harmless as Mars's iron tears.
Pilot to bombardier, we're losing
altitude. We're going down. *Mayday*,
mayday, the earth calls to us.

Mugabe's Glasses

*Indeed, his brother Donato had told me that books had been
Mugabe's only friends as a child. And Mugabe confirmed this:
"That's what my mother also used to say. Yes, I liked reading,
reading, reading every little book I found. Yes, I preferred to keep
to myself rather than playing with others. I didn't want too many
friends, one or two only—the chosen ones. I lived in my mind
a lot. I liked talking to myself, reciting little poems and so on;
reading things aloud to myself."*
~ Heidi Holland

Suppose there is forgiveness
for the father who forsakes a household,
cremates his own silhouette in the horizon's sunset,
but no pardon from the boy who knows
his father once spoke their family name to a settler,
then let it be mangled by impatient *mukiwa* lips.

There, perhaps, young Robert begins
a descent into books—the staunch
typeface that fades but never alters,
never abandons its field's black rows.
His eyes, worn weak by reading,
watch for a road-weary father,
a brother's risen corpse.

      Nothing but a setting
darkness. Mother prays,
dissolves all pain in god, the fire-
and-ice string of missionaries.
Robert, they school him,
*you'll deliver your siblings
through tomorrow's door,*
and, *Robert, a true king
wears crowns upon his eyes,
not his scalp.*

When he wakes in the cool
palace, Mugabe crowns his eyes
and reads his people as he once was—
under siege by Union Jack's shadow,
dismembered souls, intestines
thin as twine. The vision
of a liberator exact as a sniper's
scope. *Slay the ghosts*
who would concede Zimbabwe,
who'd revise its gospel.

The ghosts go unscathed by bullets,
but everywhere there is blood—
staining harvest, dyeing pages,
saying, *Robert, you are this text's*
keeper, chosen. Our author.
Our sire. You mustn't relinquish—
to be forgotten will never be forgiveness.

Dr. Imperial's Tree of Knowledge

~ after the painting of the same name by Roger Brown

A sigil of strange medicine
pressed against dusk. The serpent
entwines the smooth trunk,
constricts with a jealousy
only original ardor could ferment.

At the roots, two venomed
native lovers so succulent and splayed
—in worship—like fallen fruit.

The soil not chic enough,
their sovereign's skins now worn,
the two desire more than the sun-
bleached cloak of Empire. The pair—
meaning woman meeting
man, meaning one—
anticipates storm winds' downdrafts
carrying the snake's hexagon-coded
moltings into their net of hands.
What will they fashion of the thin hide—
new nation or new uniforms,
new ethos or new flags?

Behind the sky's dimming tarp, the clandestine
Doctor wishes to forget this history—
disremember sowing these seeds
with bloody jewels, molding those first
two serfs, and firing
their clay in his jaws' kiln.

How they once prayed
to him in a neon language with no
letters left for their own names. O,
this ungrateful reverence
of a new malice all their own.

A History of Fear

Something fled the ocean's nightmare of immersion

(terror's needle threading the cheekbone,

sealing gills). Maybe it had limbs. Maybe

it was all lack of form—a roving amoeba

in distress, run ashore by survival's

gale. *Inhale*: that searing first taste

of gaseous oxygen. *Breathe this.*

Run. No legs. *Grow them. Run.*

Motion became the frequency

Darwin would later amplify, the fittest

hearing this: *Move from here*

or you will die :: Evolution has only been

an evacuation route ran from divine wrath,

ran from the horsemen,

ran from runners who'd learned

to eat other runners. Our soles'

pedometers all set to the day

when we'll have no more strides,

when the waves that made us

return to obliterate—undertow sifting

our remains, fertilizing a deep, blue womb.

The Father Poem

~ after Jenny Napolitano and David Keplinger

We burn him and cup his ashes
with our palms. We fill sandbags.
He becomes a levee of misunderstanding—
everything he wanted in life so simple,

yet, from above, we drizzled on what was
his childless tract, we muddied
his small path that led
toward an easy spot next to god
on some protean back porch
where the lord hums and shucks kings
from his fingers. That was the father's
destiny. But our condensation
on his small pleasures
made "dad" of "man,"
and it was all over. He never stood
a chance—
            and now we take
the wet dust of his cold body
for laying a soft-cobbled wall, hoping
what's left of him will save us
from our own storm surge.
If we were kind, we would just wait
for low tide, mill the white sand
with his own grains and sculpt
the castle he could have been.

What the Rapture Will Be Like

Big white birds are walking through the mud,
and they never get dirty.
~ Brigit Pegeen Kelly

Moisture incubating
in the clouds' soft eggs.

They hatch not rain but wings
and legs spindly like the weak
skeletons of umbrellas.

The river makes a bed :: banks
bled over :: liquid evicting worms, beetles
from their sedimentary keeps.

Born birds land holy
and trudge through it all
like the Rapture's custodial
procession :: their plumage
brilliant white and awaiting
everything around them to soon rise.

My Ban-Kai

The simple fist is pure sword:
pure edge, no collar, no grip
—the body grown sharp
from knuckle to coccyx,

a chorus of joints with one
desperate note to belt through you.

This strike may finish the striker, true—
every reserve of twitching fiber
and stoic bone smelted down,
compressed into a gypsobelum stab.

The world will hear my agony, but before
bystanders would think to question
the how-why of my death,
they'd first burn to know
what on earth could have given you
such a scar. There
you would have to begin my story.

Epithalamion

~ for Conor and Missy

I know you, though not tomorrow—
our arms now to become both lifelines
and ramshackle bridges
between *here* and *after*. We take
these next paces hoping love will keep
taut until we've crossed. But enough
with forward glances—I am here
for your now, having found
the epicenter of my heartquaking—
the anxious tremors, the joy-
ful beat to which I'll walk
the rest of life.

          We have bent to pan
in each other's streams—our eyes
trained on what others abandoned
searches for lifetimes ago. What I found
in you, I shared with you and you the same.

With wonder flattening the world
once again, let us gather our gear—
sacrifice one shirt and blouse each, stitch them
hem to hem for a two-headed sail.
Against the ocean's cold slaps, we embark
pursuing a falling sun. For now,
it is ours to capture.

NOTES

Opening: Elaine Equi quoted from her poem "Second Thoughts" in the collection *Ripple Effect*. The character Butch (Bruce Willis) quoted from the film *Pulp Fiction* (1994), written and directed by Quentin Tarantino. Frantz Fanon quoted from the essay "The Black Man and Language" from *Black Skin, White Masks*. Lupe Fiasco (Wasalu Muhammad Jaco) quoted from the song "Go Go Gadget Flow" on the album *The Cool*.

"I'll See It When I Believe It": The character Ricky Bobby (Will Ferrell) quoted from the film *Talladega Nights: The Ballad of Ricky Bobby* (2006), directed by Adam McKay.

"No Passengers": Donald Barthelme quoted from the story "Among the Beanwoods," published in the *Hopkins Review* 1, no. 1.

"Sex with America": Marvin Gaye quoted from the song "Ain't That Peculiar."

"Sound Culture": Saul Bellow as quoted by Bill Moyers during a speech at the Association for Education in Journalism and Mass Communication Conference on August 9, 2007. Sidney Poitier quoted from appearance on "Larry King Live," originally aired May 11, 2008.

"Men Die Miserably for Lack": John B. Bogart quote printed on the welcome theater of the new Newseum (Washington, D.C.).

"Gazelle Theory No. 44": Quote from the Warner Brothers cartoon "Roughly Squeaking" (1946), written by Tedd Pierce and Michael Maltese, directed by Charles Jones.

"Public-Verb Agreement": Thomas Sayers Ellis quoted from the poem "Marcus Garvey Vitamins" in the collection *The Maverick Room*.

"Flight School": Joi (Joi Gilliam) quoted from the song "Gravity" on the album *Tennessee Slim Is the Bomb*.

"Mugabe's Glasses": Excerpt from the book *Dinner with Mugabe* by Heidi Holland.

"What the Rapture Will Be Like": Brigit Pegeen Kelly quoted from a personal anecdote told during a reading at the Library of Congress on April 2, 2009.

THE VQR POETRY SERIES

The VQR Poetry Series strives to publish some of the freshest, most accomplished poetry being written today. The series gathers a group of diverse poets committed to using intensely focused language to affect the way that readers see the world. A poem, at its heart, is a statement of refusal to accept common knowledge and the status quo. By studying the world for themselves, these poets illuminate what we, as a culture, may learn from close inspection.

BOOKS IN THE SERIES